FEEDING THE WORLD
Soybeans

Feeding the World

CORN
DAIRY PRODUCTS
EGGS
FARMED FISH
MEAT
RICE
SOYBEANS
WHEAT

FEEDING THE WORLD

Soybeans

JANE E. SINGER

MASON CREST

Mason Crest
450 Parkway Drive, Suite D
Broomall, PA 19008
www.masoncrest.com

Printed and bound in the United States of America.

First printing
9 8 7 6 5 4 3 2 1

Series ISBN: 978-1-4222-2741-1
ISBN: 978-1-4222-2748-0
ebook ISBN: 978-1-4222-9080-4

The Library of Congress has cataloged the

hardcopy format(s) as follows:

Library of Congress Cataloging-in-Publication Data

Singer, Jane E.
    Soybeans / Jane E. Singer.
        p. cm. — (Feeding the world)
    ISBN 978-1-4222-2748-0 (hardcover) — ISBN 978-1-4222-2741-1 (series) — ISBN 978-1-4222-9080-4 (ebook)
    1. Soybean—Juvenile literature. 2. Food supply—Juvenile literature. I. Title. II. Series: Feeding the world.
    SB205.S7S43 2014
    663'.64—dc23
                                2013004742

CONTENTS

1. Where Do Soybeans Come From?   7
2. The History of Soybeans   17
3. Who Grows the Soybeans We Eat?   23
4. How Are Soybeans Grown?   29
5. How Do Soybeans Get to Your Plate?   35
Words to Know   45
Find Out More   46
Index   47
About the Author & Picture Credits   48

CHAPTER ONE

Where Do Soybeans Come From?

What was the last thing you ate? Did you eat some meat? Or some vegetables? Maybe you had a bowl of cereal or some rice.

You could probably talk about the last meal you ate. You can say how it tasted. You can talk about how it smelled. But do you know where your food came from?

You might have pulled the cereal box from the cupboard. You might have poured milk from the fridge into your bowl. But how did those foods get to the supermarket where your family bought them?

Even though food is so important, we often don't know much about it. We might not know it grew in the ground. We might not know how far it came to get to us. Or how it got to the grocery store. There's a lot to learn about food!

FARMS

Pretty much every food starts out on a farm. Farms are where food is grown or raised. Both plants and animals come from farms.

Vegetables and fruits are plants. Plants grow in the ground on farms. Farmers must pick the fruits and vegetables.

Grains are plants too. Grains are foods like rice and oats. They are tiny seeds on certain kinds of plants. Grains grow in the ground on farms, just like fruits and vegetables.

Meat comes from animals. So do some other foods. Eggs usually come from chickens. Butter and cheese come from animal milk.

All the animals that give us meat, milk, and eggs are raised on farms too. They eat corn, grass, and other plants that grow in the ground.

Farmers are the people that work on farms. They are in charge of growing crops and raising animals. It's hard work being a farmer. But it's really important work. Without farmers, we wouldn't have food.

GROWING A GARDEN

If you really want to see where food comes from, try growing it yourself! Ask your parents if you can start a garden in your yard. Or grow some vegetables in pots if you don't have room for a whole garden. When you grow a garden, you'll see what happens to fruits and vegetables from start to finish. First, you plant seeds in some dirt. They grow into tiny plants when they get water and sunlight. Then they keep growing bigger and bigger until they produce vegetables and fruits. Then you can harvest them and eat them. And you know just where they came from!

FACTORIES

What about bread and jelly and frozen dinners? Those things didn't grow on plants! There aren't any bread trees or frozen dinner bushes.

8   **Soybeans**

All the food you can find in the supermarket has a story. Many of those stories start on a farm. Cookies may not grow on trees, but many of the ingredients in cookies did!

That might be true, but think about what those foods are made out of. The **ingredients** in all those foods come from farms. Then they are sent to a factory that makes them into a new food.

Imagine you're eating some pasta and sauce. What is it made out of? First, there's the pasta. Pasta is made out of flour, which is ground-up wheat. Wheat is a kind of grain.

The sauce is made out of tomatoes. Tomatoes grow on farms. There are onions and garlic in sauce too. Both of those are vegetables that also grow on farms. The sauce might also have herbs in it, which are plants we use to change the taste of the sauce.

Your pasta has some cheese on top. Cheese is made out of milk. Usually it's made out of cow's milk.

Finally, your pasta has meatballs on top. The meatballs are made out of meat. It could be pork or beef. In other words, it is made from pig and cow meat. And pigs and cows are raised on farms.

Soymilk is a drink made from soybeans. Many people drink soymilk instead of milk from a cow. Soybeans can be made into many different kinds of things, from milk to yogurt to cereal.

 **10** **Soybeans**

All of those ingredients go to factories. The wheat comes from a grain farm. The tomatoes, onions, and garlic come from vegetable farms. The milk for the cheese comes from a dairy farm (dairy means milk). The meat for the meatballs comes from animal farms.

The factories take all of those ingredients and make them into pasta, sauce, cheese, and meatballs. Big machines grind all of the wheat into flour. Then they mix the flour with water and other stuff to make the dough. Other machines heat up the milk and add things to it so it becomes cheese. Other factories cut the vegetables to make the sauce, and make meatballs.

At the end, all the ingredients come together into your meal. It still has to get to you, though.

STORES

Now your food has to go to the grocery store. Lots of foods are sent to grocery store warehouses first. Warehouses keep food until it's ready to be sent to the store.

Trucks, planes, trains, and boats pick up food from factories. They take the food to warehouses.

At the warehouse, people sort all the food. Some of it will be sent to a grocery store in one area. Some will be sent to a grocery store a few miles away. More will be sent to other grocery stores in other places. One of those grocery stores is the place you and your family shop.

Then, trucks come to pick up the food at the warehouse. They take it to the grocery stores.

That's the part you know already. If you've been to a grocery store, you know how it's all set up. **Customers** like you and your family buy the food they need. But they might not know just how far that food has come!

SOYBEAN STORY

Soybeans are a food that lots of people have eaten. In some parts of the world, people eat them all the time. In other places, people might not eat soybeans as often.

Lots of people who don't eat meat eat soybeans instead. Or they eat milk, yogurt, or **tofu** that is made out of soybeans.

Even if you think you've never had soybeans, you might be in for a surprise. Lots of the animals we eat as meat eat soybeans. Farmers give them food made out of soybeans. Cows, pigs, and more get fed with soybeans.

Where Do Soybeans Come From?   11

Young soybeans are green like these. In Japan, people eat green soybeans as edamame. Edamame are soybeans boiled in water with salt.

 **12   Soybeans**

Many animals around the world eat food that has soybeans in it. Animal food used on farms has soybean meal in it. Soybean meal is a kind of flour made from soybeans.

Most of the world's soybean crop ends up in animals' stomachs. So when we eat those animals, it's kind of like we're eating soybeans too!

Just like other vegetables, soybeans are grown on farms. Most of them are grown on really big farms. Farmers grow lots and lots of soybeans.

Of course, some farmers grow smaller amounts of soybeans. They might have a small farm that only grows soybeans. Or they might have a farm that grows a lot of different things. One of those things is soybeans.

Where Do Soybeans Come From?   13

Have you ever eaten tofu? Tofu is made from crushed up soybeans. Many people eat tofu instead of meat. Tofu is eaten in salads, soups, and by itself.

14 Soybeans

Soybeans are made into a lot of different things. There's soy milk. That's a drink made out of soybeans. There's soy yogurt. There's oil that comes from soybeans. Tofu is made out of soybeans. So is soy sauce. The list can go on and on!

All of those soy **products** are made in factories. Then they get sent to the grocery store. Finally, you and your family go to the store and bring them home to eat.

VEGETARIANS

People who don't eat meat are called vegetarians. People don't eat meat for a lot of reasons. Some don't like that we have to kill animals to eat them. They think that we should be kind to all animals, and that means not eating them. Other vegetarians stay away from eating meat because they think it's healthier. For some people, not eating meat makes them feel better.

Lots of vegetarians eat food made out of soybeans instead of meat. For example, they might eat tofu instead of meat.

CHAPTER TWO

The History of Soybeans

Soybeans have been around for a long time. They're an old food. They've been around in some countries for thousands of years. Not every country has known about soybeans for so long, though. In some parts of the world, soybeans weren't always the important food they are today.

THE FIRST SOYBEANS

Soybeans first grew in China thousands of years ago. They grew only in the wild back then. But people figured out that they were good to eat. They decided it was a good idea to grow them on farms.

On farms, people could grow lots of soybeans. They would always know where the soybeans were. They wouldn't have to walk very far to get to them. In the wild, people never knew where they would find soybeans, and they might be far away from villages.

Did you know that soy sauce is made from soybeans? You might have had soy sauce on rice or other foods. Like many other foods, that soy sauce started as soybeans growing on a farm.

 **18** **Soybeans**

Soybeans were growing in China by at least the 11th century BCE. That's a long time ago!

In China, soybeans were one of the most important foods around. People believed that soybeans were one of five **sacred** grains. Rice is another sacred grain. All together, the sacred grains helped feed people and keep them alive.

The Chinese may have been the first to start growing soybeans, but soon other people were growing soybeans, too. Other groups of people in Asia began growing soybeans. Pretty soon, soybeans were growing in countries like Japan, Indonesia, Thailand, and India.

People ate soybeans fresh. They ate them dried. They also ate them pickled. **Pickling** is a way to keep fresh food longer. You might be familiar with pickles, which are cucumbers that have been pickled. Soybeans can be pickled too.

For a long time, soybeans stayed in Asia. Other people didn't know about growing or eating them. It would be a little longer before the rest of the world knew about soybeans.

SOYBEANS AROUND THE WORLD

Little by little, soybeans made their way to the rest of the world. People from other places who visited Asia ate them. They brought seeds back to their homes.

Some plant scientists in Europe started studying soybeans. At least one German scientist wrote about soybeans in 1712. There were even a few soybean plants growing in France in the 1700s.

In the United States, some farmers started planting soybeans as food for their animals in the 1800s. But not many people ate the soybeans themselves.

Soybeans still weren't very popular outside of Asia for many years. It wasn't until the 1900s that people around the world really started eating them.

In the early 1900s, a scientist in the United States found that soybeans have a lot of **protein**. We need to eat protein to be strong and healthy. Eating meat is another way to get a lot of protein. People started eating more soybeans when they found out how healthy soybeans were.

Farmers tested out ways to grow soybeans. In some parts of Europe and the Americas, they grew really well. But most of the soybean plants grown outside of Asia were still fed to animals.

Slowly, people figured out soybeans were a good thing to eat. And farmers saw soybeans were good to grow. More and more countries grew soybeans.

In Japan, tofu is often eaten in miso soup. Small tofu squares float in the brown or yellow soup. Tofu is just one of many foods made from soybeans.

20   **Soybeans**

In the past few years, lots of people have started eating more soybeans. They eat them in tofu and drink soymilk. They use soy sauce and soybean oil.

Today, soybeans grow all over the world. And people enjoy them from China to Brazil to Canada.

NOT JUST FOR FOOD

Soybeans have been used for things besides food. Soybeans have a lot of oil in them. People can eat the oil, but it can be used in other stuff too. Soybean oil is put into paint and ink and even crayons! It can be used to power cars and other machines instead of gasoline. Chances are, you've used something with soy in it.

CHAPTER THREE

Who Grows the Soybeans We Eat?

Farmers all around the world are growing soybeans. They're growing more soybeans than ever before. Every year, there are more soybeans growing than the year before.

Lots of soybeans mean lots of farmers. They all are looking for the best ways to grow soybeans, no matter where they live.

THE FARMERS

The people who grow soybeans are just like people who grow other things we eat—they're farmers!

Farmers have a lot of work to do. They plant seeds. They water the seeds. They take care of the seedlings. And they harvest the vegetables in the end.

This farm is growing both soybeans and wheat. Many smaller farms grow more than one kind of plant. On bigger farms, farmers may choose just to grow wheat or soybeans, instead of both.

Farmers might also fix tractors. They keep track of all the money the farm makes. Farmers have to find places to sell their soybeans. They also have to find workers to help them grow and pick the soybeans.

Some farmers work on very small farms. They only grow enough food for themselves and their families.

These kinds of farmers probably grow a lot of different kinds of plants. They might grow soybeans. But they also grow corn and carrots and potatoes and more. They don't farm to make money. They farm to eat.

Other farmers have huge farms. There are thousands of rows of plants. All the plants are the same kind. Big machines are used to plant and pick the soybeans.

Then there are farmers who have farms that are in between. They aren't tiny, but they aren't huge.

Most soybean farmers work on big farms. All they grow is soybeans. They have figured out how to grow a lot of them really well.

24   Soybeans

More than one out of three soybeans in the world is grown in the United States on farms like this. The United States grows more soybeans than any other country.

BY COUNTRY

The country that grows the most soybeans in the world is the United States. That might be a surprise, since the United States didn't grow many soybeans 100 years ago. But today, farmers in the United States grow a lot of them!

Soybeans are a very important **crop** in the United States. Corn is the only crop the United States grows more than soybeans.

Most of the soybeans grown in the United States are eaten by animals. Lots of them are also made into soybean oil.

The United States grows more soybeans than people can use in the country. So it sells them to other countries. For example, China buys a lot of soybeans from the United States.

Who Grows the Soybeans We Eat? 25

Farmers in Argentina grow a huge number of soybeans. Only the United States and Brazil grow more soybeans than Argentina. This Argentinean soybean farm has thousands of soybean plants.

 **26 Soybeans**

Brazil isn't far behind the United States. Brazil grows the second-biggest amount of soybeans in the world. It also sells a lot of them to other countries that want more soybeans.

Brazil might soon grow the most soybeans in the world. There's a lot of land left in Brazil that could become soybean farms.

Next is Argentina. Together with Brazil and a few other countries, Argentina is helping to make South America one of the most important places for soybean farms.

China still grows a lot of soybeans too. It is the fourth-biggest soybean grower in the world. Thousands of years after they started growing soybeans, Chinese farmers are still growing them.

Other countries that grow a lot of soybeans include India, Paraguay, Canada, and Italy. Soybeans grow all over the world!

CHAPTER FOUR

How Are Soybeans Grown?

J ust like other plants we eat, soybeans grow on farms. The farmer helps them grow from seed to soybean. So how does she do it?

SEEDS

Soybeans are actually seeds. If you planted a soybean, it could grow into a soybean plant. Eating seeds isn't unusual. Corn is a seed (and so is popcorn). We also eat sunflower seeds, pumpkin seeds, and more.

Farmers can plant dried soybeans in the ground. They will grow into new soybean plants.

Sometimes farmers have to prepare the farm first. They have to make sure the farm is ready to grow the soybeans.

The farmer will use a tractor to make long rows to plant the seeds in. Then he might use another tractor to actually plant the seeds. Or he might do it by hand, if it's a small farm.

Soybeans need warm weather to grow. They don't grow in very cold places. They also don't grow in the winter in places with cold winters.

Farmers in each country have learned when to plant soybeans. They usually plant them in the spring. Then the plants have a warm summer to grow. By the time it gets cooler again, the plants have grown and have made the soybeans!

GROW YOUR OWN

You don't have to be a farmer to grow your own soybeans. You can also ask your paretns to grow them at home! You can plant them in a garden in the ground. You can also plant them in pots if you don't have a yard. In the spring, plant soybeans about two inches into the dirt. Plant the seeds at least three inches apart. Keep the dirt wet and make sure your garden or pot is in the sun. When seedlings pop up, keep watering whenever the dirt gets dry. Watch as your plants grow soybean pods. You can pick the pods when they are green and as long as your finger. Then cook them and enjoy your hard work!

Each soybean you eat is a seed. If you plant a soybean, it could grow into a soybean plant. When soybeans are fully grown and dry, they turn from green to this yellow or brown color.

30   **Soybeans**

Soybean plants start as these very small seedlings. At first, they have just a few leaves and no soybeans. In many soybean fields, thousands of beans grow next to each other in rows like these.

GROWING UP

Once the seeds are planted, the farmer waits. Pretty soon, tiny seedlings poke out of the dirt. At first they have two leaves each. Then they grow more and more leaves.

Farmers have to protect the seedlings as they grow. Animals and bugs might want to eat the seedlings. The farmer has a few choices to protect his crops.

He could put up a fence for bigger animals. The fence will keep the animals away from the soybeans.

But fences won't keep out bugs. Most farmers use pesticides. Pesticides are chemicals that kill bugs.

Weeds can also get in the way. Weeds are any plants that a farmer doesn't want growing near soybeans. Weeds will steal the water and **nutrients** in the soil away from the soybeans.

A farmer might use more chemicals to get rid of weeds. Or she might have people pull them out by hand.

Watering fields of soybean plants would be a lot of work for farmers to do themselves. Instead of watering each plant one at a time, some farmers use these large sprinklers. That way, they can water many plants at once.

 **Soybeans**

When it's time to harvest their soybeans, farmers use machines called combine harvesters. First, combine harvesters pull the soybean plants from the ground. Then, they pull the soybeans from the rest of the plant.

After some time, the seedling becomes a plant with lots of leaves. It even has flowers. The flowers are white or purple.

Then the flowers turn into the soybeans. The soybeans grow in fat, green **pods**. The pods are fuzzy on the outside.

Inside the pods are soybeans. There are two, three, or four soybeans inside each pod.

HARVESTING

The final step on the farm is to pick all those soybeans. The farmer has a choice. She can pick fresh soybeans or she can pick dry soybeans.

Once combine harvesters have pulled the soybeans from the rest of the soybean plant, the beans have to be moved. Here, a combine harvester is dropping the soybeans into a tractor.

 **34** **Soybeans**

Fresh soybeans are the ones you eat. They are green. The pods are still green. It doesn't take as long to grow fresh soybeans. Once the pods are nice and fat, the farmer can pick them.

Most farmers pick dry soybeans. They just wait longer. The leaves on the soybean plant start to turn yellow. The leaves die.

As the leaves die, they fall off. Underneath are the soybean pods! Inside are dried soybeans.

Farmers with small farms might pick the soybeans by hand. But most farmers use big machines to do it. The machines are called combines.

Combines also take the soybeans out of their pods. If the farmer doesn't have a combine, he has to take the beans out of the pod by hand.

Once they're harvested, soybeans are ready for the next step in their journey.

ORGANIC GROWING

Lots of farmers use chemicals to help their crops grow. They put chemicals in the dirt to add nutrients. The nutrients help plants grow bigger and faster. Farmers might also put chemicals on the ground to kill weeds or on the plants to kill bugs. But some farmers don't want to use chemicals. The chemicals can pollute the ground and nearby water. They can also make animals and even people sick. So, instead of using chemicals, some farmers grow things organically. That means they don't use chemicals at all. They use nature instead. For example, an organic farmer uses compost to make the dirt healthier, not chemicals. Compost is just recycled plants. A farmer will put all his dead plants and weeds into a pile. Then, it breaks down and becomes what looks like really dark dirt at the end. That's compost! The farmer puts compost around his plants, and it helps them grow. There aren't any chemicals involved at all.

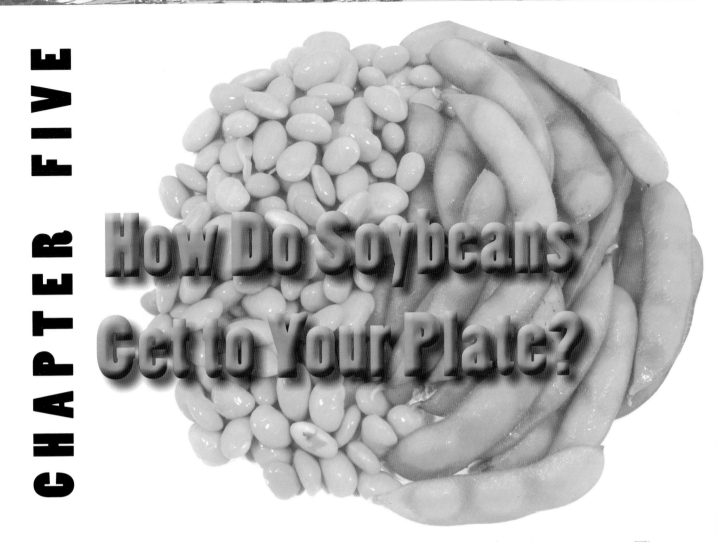

CHAPTER FIVE

How Do Soybeans Get to Your Plate?

A fter the farmer has planted, grown, and picked her soybeans, they're ready to move on. The soybeans go to a factory. They are taken there by trucks.

MOVING SOYBEANS AROUND

Every time the soybeans move from place to place, someone has to do the moving. First the soybeans moved from the farm to storage. Then they moved to a factory. Next, they moved to a warehouse and on to a grocery store. Finally, they made it to your home.

Soybeans can move a really big distance. Soybeans may have been grown 1,000 miles from where they ended up. They may have been grown on the other side of the world!

How do soybeans get from one place to another? Trucks, trains, planes, and boats! If they aren't going very far, soybeans might travel in a big truck. It might be faster to put them in a train, plane, or boat if they have to go really far.

After soybeans have been harvested, they have to be moved. Large trucks carry soybeans from the farm to the factory. Once the soybeans are ready for the store, trucks move the soybeans again.

And lots of soybeans do have to go really far. People in lots of countries eat foods with soybeans in them. But not all countries grow soybeans. If you live in Australia, you probably eat soybeans from China. If you live in Canada, you eat soybeans from the United States or Brazil. Those soybeans have a long way to travel. People would use planes or boats to move soybeans around that far.

After the soybeans are taken from the farm to the factory, soybeans are processed. Remember, processed means to be made into something new. In factories, soybeans can become a lot of different things.

DRYING

Soybeans have to be as dry as they can possibly be. Water in soybeans will make them get moldy.

Even if a farmer has harvested dry soybeans, they're still a little wet. They have to get even drier.

Soybeans can dry in the air. They are just spread out on the floor in the sun. It takes a week or two for them to dry out.

Soybeans can be dried in large machines before being stored in silos like these. Without machines like these, farmers had to wait for their soybeans to dry in the sun.

The soybeans can also dry in a machine. They are put under a big air dryer. The air is warm. The soybeans dry very quickly.

CLEANING UP

If the soybeans are going to be turned into food, they have to be clean. We don't want dirt or bugs in our food!

Special machines are used for cleaning soybeans. They don't use water, though. That would make the soybeans wet. And the farmer just went through all that trouble to dry them out.

SOY OIL AND MEAL

Most soybeans are made into soybean oil and soybean **meal**. Both come out of the same soybeans.

In the factory, the soybeans are cracked open. They are mixed up and rolled around for a while.

All that mixing makes it easy to get out the oil. All soybeans have a lot of oil in them. The factory can press the soybeans flat to get out the oil. Or it can use special chemicals that pull out the oil.

Then, the oil goes to different factories. Those factories mix the oil with other ingredients to make new foods for us to eat.

After the oil is taken out, what's left is dried-up soybean parts. They are cut up and mixed up even more. They become soybean meal. A lot of soybean meal is used to feed animals. The soybean meal is sent to animal farmers. They use it as a food for cows, pigs, and other animals.

This happens to almost all the soybeans grown in the world. Out of all the soybeans in the world, 85 percent get made into soybean oil and soybean meal. That means that out of 100 bags of soybeans, 85 of them are made into oil and meal.

SOYMILK

Some soybeans become soymilk. You can drink it if you can't drink milk. Soymilk doesn't taste exactly like milk from animals. Lots of people like the taste of soymilk.

Factories make soymilk by grinding up soybeans and mixing them with water. Then they take out the bits of soybean. What's left is soymilk.

Some soymilk is flavored. The factories add chocolate or vanilla or other flavors. Sometimes, factories add vitamins to soymilk to make it healthier. Some soymilk has sugar in it.

Soybeans are made into many different kinds of food. Soybeans are made into soy sauce, soymilk, cereal, tofu, and many other things. You might be eating or drinking something made of soybeans without even knowing it!

After everything is added, the soymilk is put into packages. The packaging helps make sure that germs don't get into the soymilk. Packaging helps the soymilk stay good longer.

TOFU

Have you ever eaten tofu? Some people eat it all the time. Other people have never tried it.

Tofu is made out of soybeans. Some vegetarians eat tofu instead of meat. Sometimes people just like the taste of it.

Tofu starts out as soymilk. Then the factory adds in some other ingredients. The ingredients make the soymilk thick. It splits into watery stuff and solid stuff. The watery stuff is poured out. All that's left is the solid, called bean curd.

The factory collects all the solid curd and presses it together really hard. After it is pressed, the curd turns into a block of tofu.

There are different kinds of tofu. Firm tofu can be cut and hold its shape. It doesn't have much water in it. The factory pressed out a lot of the liquid from the tofu.

Next time you're eating soybeans or something made from soybeans, think about the story of your food. A lot of people had to work hard to make sure you could eat those soybeans!

 **42** **Soybeans**

THE GROCERY STORE

Now the soybeans we started with could be lots of things. They could be a bottle of soybean oil. They could be fresh soybeans. They could be soymilk or tofu.

All those new foods have to get to the grocery store. From factories, the soybean foods are sent to warehouses. Grocery stores own the warehouses.

At the warehouse, the food gets sorted. Some of it will go to one grocery store. Some will go to another. The soybeans can get sent to lots and lots of different stores.

The grocery store your family shops at gets some of the soybean foods. Workers unpack them and put them on shelves.

That's where you come in! You and your family come to the store. You could buy tofu, or vegetable oil, or meat. All those foods have soybeans in them.

DIFFERENT KINDS OF SEEDS

Not all soybeans are the same. Some are better for eating fresh. Some are better for soymilk. And some are better for drying out and using to make oil and meal. You can tell by the color of the soybean seed. Green soybeans are the best for eating. Yellow ones are made into soymilk and tofu. Black soybeans are used for oil and meal. If you ever eat a whole soybean (often called edamame), it will be green.

THE PEOPLE

Another important part of getting the soybeans to you is all the people! The farmer is one person who helps soybeans along.

Truck drivers, pilots, and others move soybeans around the world. They move them on trucks, planes, boats, and trains from farms to factories to you.

Workers at the factory help too. They fix machines that break. They unpack the soybeans that come to the factory. They test the food to make sure it's safe for people to eat.

At the grocery store, workers put the soybean foods on the shelves. They check out customers at the register.

All those people help get soybeans to you! Without them, you probably would never eat a soybean or a food with soybeans in it.

Next time you're at the grocery store, keep an eye out for soybeans. The store might sell them fresh next to the other vegetables. Soybeans could be in that bottle of vegetable oil. The animals the meat came from probably ate some soybeans. And there will probably be a lot of soymilk in the cooler near the animal milk.

Think about where all those soybeans came from. Lots of people helped grow and process them. There were a lot of steps in the trip from the farm to your plate. And at the end, you got to eat tasty soybeans!

 **44** **Soybeans**

WORDS TO KNOW:

crop: A fruit or vegetable grown for food.

customers: People who buy things, including food.

ingredients: Foods that are mixed with others to make new foods.

meal: A kind of flour made by grinding and crushing a plant (like soybeans).

nutrients: Chemicals that living things need to eat in food to stay healthy.

pickling: Making food last longer by keeping it in a jar or container filled with vinegar (or other liquids).

pods: The covering around beans.

products: Things people make, buy, and sell.

protein: A part of food that helps build strong muscles and keep people healthy. Meat, milk, and other dairy products have a lot of protein.

sacred: Very important to a group of people, sometimes because of religion.

tofu: A soft food made from soybeans, usually served in white blocks.

FOR MORE INFO

ONLINE

Tiki's Guide to Food
tiki.oneworld.net/food/home.html

Pod to Plate
www.podtoplate.org

Quiz: Where Does this Food Come From?
www.1millionacts.com.au/inspiration/kids/quiz/where/does/this/food/come/from

IN BOOKS

Bial, Raymond. *The Super Soybean*. Morton Grove, Ill.: Albert Whitman and Company, 2007.

Gibbons, Gail. *The Vegetables We Eat*. New York: Holiday House, 2007.

Reilly, Kathleen M. Food: *25 Amazing Projects*. White River Junction, Ver.: Nomad Press, 2010.

INDEX

Argentina: 26, 27
Asia: 19

Brazil: 21, 27, 38

chemicals: 31, 35, 40
China: 17, 19, 21, 25, 27, 38

factories: 8, 11, 15, 38, 40–41, 43
farm: 8–9, 11, 13, 17, 24, 27, 29, 35, 43
farmer: 8, 11, 13, 19, 23–25, 27, 29–33, 35, 37–40, 43

garden: 8, 30
grains: 8, 19
grocery store: 7, 11, 15, 37, 43–44

harvest: 8, 22, 33–35, 38

ingredients: 9, 11, 40–41

meat: 7–9, 11, 14, 15, 19, 41, 43–44

organic: 35

protein: 19

scientists: 19
seedlings: 23, 30, 31
seeds: 8, 19, 23, 29–31, 43
soymilk: 10, 21, 40–41, 43–44
soy oil: 40

tofu: 11, 14–15, 20, 21, 41, 43
tractors: 23
trucks: 11, 37, 38, 43

United States: 19, 25–27, 38

vegetables: 7–9, 11, 13, 23, 44
vegetarians: 15, 41

warehouses: 11, 43

ABOUT THE AUTHOR

Jane E. Singer is freelance writer with several titles to her name. Singer writes about health, history, and other topics that affect young people. She is passionate about learning in and out of the classroom.

PICTURE CREDITS